THE
MAN
IN THE
MIRROR

INSPIRATIONAL QUOTES FOR MEN OF ALL AGES

I0170462

CURT THOMAS

WWW.CURTTHOMASSPEAKS.COM

THE MAN IN THE MIRROR

ISBN: 978-0-9961977-3-1

Library of Congress Control Number: 2015904059

CURT THOMAS UNLIMITED, LLC Orangeburg, SC

WWW.CURTTHOMASSPEAKS.COM

The MAN in the MIRROR

DEDICATION

This Book is dedicated to my father Albert Thomas. If it wasn't for you, there would be no me. You have shown my brother Bernard and I what a real man looks like. You will always be my hero and my reason for my being. All that I am is and always will be because of you! I love you...

Thank you "Pop"...

To my brother Bernard, I have watched you grow into a man. You have overcome so many obstacles in life. I'm proud of you man. Never stop achieving! I love you...

Thank you bro...

To my seeds: Tyler, Preston, and Michael...Daddy loves you! I'm proud to be your father. All I do is for you!

To every grandfather, father, son, uncle, husband who is in the struggle or successes of life, may this book serve as an inspiration to you all! It's not easy being a man but never give up hope. Let your light sign bright for our future!

www.CurtThomasSpeaks.com

The MAN in the MIRROR

QUOTES

The MAN in the MIRROR

"A PATIENT MAN WILL
EAT RIPE FRUIT."

—AFRICAN PROVERB

"THE GREATER THE
POWER, THE MORE
DANGEROUS THE
ABUSE."

—EDMUND BURKE

"THE GREATEST DECEPTION MEN SUFFER IS FROM THEIR OWN OPINIONS."

—LEONARDO DA VINCI

"IT'S NOT EASY BEING A MAN. ESPECIALLY WHEN YOU HAVE A HEART THAT'S UNEASY AT TIMES."

—CURT THOMAS

"WITHOUT FEELINGS
OF RESPECT, WHAT IS
THERE TO DISTINGUISH
MEN FROM BEASTS?"

—CONFUCIUS

"MEN ARE LIKE STEEL.
WHEN THEY LOSE
THEIR TEMPER, THEY
LOSE THEIR WORTH"

—CHUCK NORRIS

"MAN BECOMES GREAT EXACTLY IN THE DEGREE IN WHICH HE WORKS FOR THE WELFARE OF HIS FELLOW-MEN."

—MAHATMA GANDHI

"MEN ARE MORE EASILY GOVERNED THROUGH THEIR VICES THAN THROUGH THEIR VIRTUES."

—NAPOLEON BONAPARTE

"IT DOESN'T TAKE MUCH TO PLEASE US MEN. WE DON'T NEED DIAMONDS AND PEARLS. JUST FEED US, BE INTIMATE WITH US FROM TIME TO TIME, AND LET US KNOW THAT YOU APPRECIATE US! THAT DOES A LOT FOR US GUYS! IT KEEPS US HOME TOO!"

—CURT THOMAS

"Men do not quit playing because they grow old; they grow old because they quit playing."

—Oliver Wendell Holmes, Sr.

"WISE MEN SPEAK BECAUSE THEY HAVE SOMETHING TO SAY; FOOLS BECAUSE THEY HAVE TO SAY SOMETHING."

—PLATO

"NEARLY ALL MEN CAN STAND ADVERSITY, BUT IF YOU WANT TO TEST A MAN'S CHARACTER, GIVE HIM POWER."

—ABRAHAM LINCOLN

"MANY MEN GO FISHING ALL OF THEIR LIVES WITHOUT KNOWING THAT IT IS NOT FISH THEY ARE AFTER."

—HENRY DAVID THOREAU

"MASTERING OTHERS
IS STRENGTH.
MASTERING YOURSELF
IS TRUE POWER."

—LAO TZU

"My sons are the reason I push myself each day! Women come and go but our seeds are with us forever."

—Curt Thomas

"IF YOU LEARN HOW
TO FORGIVE OTHERS
FOR NOT BEING
STRONG, THEN PEOPLE
CAN LEARN HOW TO
FORGIVE YOU FOR
YOUR OWN ISSUES."

—T. D. JAKES

"IT IS EASIER TO BUILD STRONG CHILDREN THAN TO REPAIR BROKEN MEN."

—FREDERICK DOUGLASS

"I FELT OBLIGATED AS THE OLDER BROTHER TO MY YOUNGER BROTHER BERNARD TO GIVE HIM INSPIRATION. I FELT IT WAS NECESSARY TO LET HIM SEE ME SUCCESSFUL SO HE CAN DO THE SAME WITH WHATEVER TALENT OR DREAM HE WISHES. IT'S WAS GREAT TO SEE HIM SURPASS ME IN EDUCATION. BUT HE STILL HAS A LONG WAY TO GO TO CATCH UP WITH ME(SMILING)."

—CURT THOMAS

"IF YOU TAKE RESPONSIBILITY FOR YOURSELF YOU WILL DEVELOP A HUNGER TO ACCOMPLISH YOUR DREAMS."

—LES BROWN

"BEING DEEPLY LOVED BY SOMEONE GIVES YOU STRENGTH, WHILE LOVING SOMEONE DEEPLY GIVES YOU COURAGE."

— LAO TZU

"GETTING A DIVORCE FELT LIKE GOING TO A FUNERAL. AFTERWARDS IT FELT LIKE I WAS LIVING IN A GRAVE. I MUST CONFESS, I'M NOT SURE IF A PERSON REALLY 'GETS OVER IT'."

—CURT THOMAS

"PATIENCE PUTS A CROWN ON THE HEAD."

—UGANDAN PROVERB

"You don't get what you want in life. You get who you are!"

—Les Brown

"IF A MAN HAS NOT DISCOVERED SOMETHING THAT HE WILL DIE FOR, HE ISN'T FIT TO LIVE."

—MARTIN LUTHER KING, JR.

IF WE KEEP DOING
WHAT WE'RE DOING,
WE'RE GOING TO KEEP
GETTING WHAT WE'RE
GETTING.

—STEPHEN COVEY

"THE WEALTH WHICH
ENSLAVES THE OWNER
ISN'T WEALTH.

—YORUBA PROVERB

"MEN ALWAYS WANT
TO BE A WOMAN'S
FIRST LOVE - WOMEN
LIKE TO BE A MAN'S
LAST ROMANCE."

—OSCAR WILDE

"THE ONLY THING THAT COMES TO A SLEEPING MAN IS DREAMS."

—TUPAC SHAKUR

"YOU WERE BORN TO WIN, BUT TO BE A WINNER, YOU MUST PLAN TO WIN, PREPARE TO WIN, AND EXPECT TO WIN."

—ZIG ZIGLAR

"MOST MEN WON'T
CONFESS THAT THEY
HAVE SMALL FEARS OF
NEVER BEING GOOD
ENOUGH."

—CURT THOMAS

"THERE ARE ONLY TWO
FORCES THAT UNITE
MEN - FEAR AND
INTEREST."

—NAPOLEON BONAPARTE

"WE CAN EASILY FORGIVE A CHILD WHO IS AFRAID OF THE DARK; THE REAL TRAGEDY OF LIFE IS WHEN MEN ARE AFRAID OF THE LIGHT."

—PLATO

"IT IS EASIER TO FIND MEN WHO WILL VOLUNTEER TO DIE, THAN TO FIND THOSE WHO ARE WILLING TO ENDURE PAIN WITH PATIENCE."

—JULIUS CAESAR

"MEN ARE LIKE WINE -
SOME TURN TO
VINEGAR, BUT THE
BEST IMPROVE WITH
AGE."

—POPE JOHN XXIII

"MY FATHER'S FATHER WAS NOT IN HIS LIFE WHEN HE WAS A CHILD. HE MADE A PROMISE TO HIMSELF NOT TO DO THE SAME TO MY BROTHER AND I. IT MADE THE DIFFERENCE IN OUR LIVES!"

—CURT THOMAS

"I AM HOPING THAT IN THIS YEAR OF THE FAMILY WE WILL GO INTO OUR FAMILIES AND RECONCILE DIFFERENCES."

—LOUIS FARRAKHAN

"YOU CAN CRY, AIN'T
NO SHAME IN IT."

—WILL SMITH

"A HAPPY MAN MARRIES THE GIRL HE LOVES, BUT A HAPPIER MAN LOVES THE GIRL HE MARRIES."

—AFRICAN PROVERB

"TO ME, IT DOESN'T MATTER WHAT YOU DO FOR A LIVING, WHITE COLLAR OR BLUE, WE MEN ALL FACE THE SAME CHALLENGES! IT AIN'T EASY BEING A MAN."

—CURT THOMAS

"WHEN LIFE KNOCKS YOU DOWN, TRY TO LAND ON YOUR BACK. BECAUSE IF YOU CAN LOOK UP, YOU CAN GET UP. LET YOUR REASON GET YOU BACK UP."

—LES BROWN

"THE ULTIMATE MEASURE OF A MAN IS NOT WHERE HE STANDS IN MOMENTS OF COMFORT AND CONVENIENCE, BUT WHERE HE STANDS AT TIMES OF CHALLENGE AND CONTROVERSY."

—MARTIN LUTHER KING, JR.

"Curt, always keep God first in your life and everything else will fall in place."

—Albert Thomas (Father)

"THOSE WHO DARE TO FAIL MISERABLY CAN ACHIEVE GREATLY."

—JOHN F. KENNEDY

"Women are the real reason we get up every day. I'm talking about real men. If there were no women, I would not even have to bathe, because why would I care? These are guys I'm hanging with. I wake up for a woman every day of my life to make it happen for her."

—Steve Harvey

"DON'T LET SOMEONE ELSE'S OPINION OF YOU BECOME YOUR REALITY."

—LES BROWN

"No individual has any right to come into the world and go out of it without leaving behind him distinct and legitimate reasons for having passed through it."

—George Washington Carver

"HOWEVER LONG THE NIGHT, THE DAWN WILL BREAK."

—AFRICAN PROVERB

"You have competition every day because you set such high standards for yourself that you have to go out every day and live up to that."

—Michael Jordan

"MY FATHER WILL ALWAYS BE MY HERO AND MY REASON FOR MY BEING WHO I AM."

—CURT THOMAS

"FORGIVE YOURSELF
FOR YOUR FAULTS AND
YOUR MISTAKES AND
MOVE ON."

—LES BROWN

"NOBODY CAN GIVE
YOU FREEDOM.
NOBODY CAN GIVE YOU
EQUALITY OR JUSTICE
OR ANYTHING. IF
YOU'RE A MAN, YOU
TAKE IT."

—MALCOLM X

"I LOOK AT OTHER MEN AS THOUGH THEY HAVE THE SAME STRUGGLES AS I DO. I VIEW THEM AS BROTHERS AND NOT MY ENEMY!"

—CURT THOMAS

"EFFORTS AND COURAGE ARE NOT ENOUGH WITHOUT PURPOSE AND DIRECTION."

—JOHN F. KENNEDY

"IF YOU'RE WALKING DOWN THE RIGHT PATH AND YOU'RE WILLING TO KEEP WALKING, EVENTUALLY YOU'LL MAKE PROGRESS."

—PRESIDENT BARACK OBAMA

"IF WOMEN KNEW THE WEIGHT WE MEN CARRY WHILE TRYING TO BE A FATHER, HUSBAND, OR LEADER THEY WOULDN'T GIVE US A HARD-TIME AT THE WRONG-TIME."

—CURT THOMAS

"WE CAN'T HELP EVERYONE, BUT EVERYONE CAN HELP SOMEONE."

—RONALD REAGAN

"MY FATHER INSTILLED IN ME TO TAKE CARE OF MY FAMILY. SHOW UP EVEN WHEN YOU DON'T WANT TO SHOW UP."

—STEVE HARVEY

"It takes courage to grow up and become who you really are."

—E.E. Cummings

"I never thought I'd suffer from depression or even contemplated suicide until I went through my divorce. Even strong men suffer from hidden emotions. However, my kids gave me a reason to live again and to bounce back! Now I take it day by day. I don't mind being candid when speaking to men at a men's conference about 'life'. That Superman Mentality won't heal you, confronting your emotions will."

—Curt Thomas

"HAVING SOMEWHERE
TO GO IS HOME.
HAVING SOMEONE TO
LOVE IS FAMILY.
HAVING BOTH IS A
BLESSING."

—UNKNOWN

"POWER DOESN'T CORRUPT PEOPLE, PEOPLE CORRUPT POWER."

—WILLIAM GADDIS

"If you have no critics you'll likely have no success."

—Malcolm X

"MY FAILURES ARE
SIMPLY PARABLES FOR
THE ENLIGHTENMENT
OF OTHERS."

—CURT THOMAS

"YOU DROWN NOT BY FALLING INTO A RIVER, BUT BY STAYING SUBMERGED IN IT."

—PAULO COELHO

"MONEY CAN'T TALK,
YET IT CAN MAKE LIES
LOOK TRUE.

—SOUTH AFRICAN
PROVERB

"No matter the circumstances that you may be going through, just push through it."

—Ray Lewis

"POWER IS ALWAYS DANGEROUS. POWER ATTRACTS THE WORST AND CORRUPTS THE BEST."

—EDWARD ABBEY

"SOME PEOPLE WANT
IT TO HAPPEN, SOME
WISH IT WOULD
HAPPEN, OTHERS
MAKE IT HAPPEN."

—MICHAEL JORDAN

"YOU MUST RECOGNIZE THAT THE WAY TO GET THE GOOD OUT OF YOUR BROTHER AND YOUR SISTER IS NOT TO RETURN EVIL FOR EVIL."

—LOUIS FARRAKHAN

"IN FAMILY LIFE, LOVE IS THE OIL THAT EASES FRICTION, THE CEMENT THAT BINDS CLOSER TOGETHER, AND THE MUSIC THAT BRINGS HARMONY.

—FRIEDRICH NIETZCHE

"MY JOB IS NOT TO REPRESENT WASHINGTON TO YOU, BUT TO REPRESENT YOU TO WASHINGTON."

—PRESIDENT BARACK OBAMA

"IF THERE IS NO ENEMY
WITHIN, THE ENEMY
OUTSIDE CAN DO YOU
NO HARM."

— AFRICAN PROVERB

"SOMETIMES A DIVORCE ISN'T ALWAYS THE MAN'S FAULT BUT MOST OF US WILL TAKE THE BLAME. WE ARE NOT ALL DOGS."

—CURT THOMAS

"IF YOU START BY
PROMISING WHAT YOU
DON'T EVEN HAVE YET,
YOU'LL LOSE YOUR
DESIRE TO WORK
TOWARDS GETTING IT."

—PAULO COELHO

"IF YOU CLEAN YOUR
BODY OUT SO THAT IT IS
NOT FIGHTING AGAINST
YOU, YOU REST BETTER,
THINK BETTER AND
YOU'RE ALWAYS LIGHT
ON YOUR FEET."

—RAY LEWIS

"I KNOW ENOUGH TO KNOW THAT NO WOMAN SHOULD EVER MARRY A MAN WHO HATED HIS MOTHER."

— MARTHA GELLHORN

"NO WOMAN WANTS TO BE IN SUBMISSION TO A MAN WHO ISN'T IN SUBMISSION TO GOD!"

— T.D. JAKES

"SEX DOESN'T KEEP A MAN AT HOME, BUT SHOWING HIM APPRECIATION WITH GOOD FOOD AND GOOD SEX WILL."

—CURT THOMAS

"IT'S NOT THE MEN IN YOUR LIFE THAT MATTERS, IT'S THE LIFE IN YOUR MEN."

— MAE WEST

"EVERY CHILD NEEDS THEIR FATHER IN THEIR LIVES! I WISH MORE MOTHER REALIZED THIS!"

— CURT THOMAS

"WHEN IN A RELATIONSHIP, A REAL MAN DOESN'T MAKE HIS WOMAN JEALOUS OF OTHERS, HE MAKES OTHERS JEALOUS OF HIS WOMAN."

— STEVE MARABOLI

"MEN DON'T SETTLE DOWN BECAUSE OF THE RIGHT WOMAN. THEY SETTLE DOWN BECAUSE THEY ARE FINALLY READY FOR IT."

— LAURELL K. HAMILTON

"ALWAYS ANTICIPATE
SEX WITH YOUR WIFE,
STAY FRESH(HYGIENE).
YOU NEVER KNOW
WHEN SHE MIGHT
CHANGE HER MIND."

—CURT THOMAS

"IF A MAN HASN'T
WHAT'S NECESSARY TO
MAKE A WOMAN LOVE
HIM, IT'S HIS FAULT,
NOT HERS."

— W. SOMERSET MAUGHAM

"YOU MUST ACT AS IF IT IS IMPOSSIBLE TO FAIL."

—ASHANTI PROVERB

"IN CASE YOU NEVER GET A SECOND CHANCE: DON'T BE AFRAID!" "AND WHAT IF YOU DO GET A SECOND CHANCE?" "YOU TAKE IT!"

— C. JOYBELL C.

"NOTHING CAN STOP THE MAN WITH THE RIGHT MENTAL ATTITUDE FROM ACHIEVING HIS GOAL; NOTHING ON EARTH CAN HELP THE MAN WITH THE WRONG MENTAL ATTITUDE."

— THOMAS JEFFERSON

"THOSE WHOM WE MOST LOVE ARE OFTEN THE MOST ALIEN TO US."

—CHRISTOPHER PAOLINI

"I BELIEVE THAT THE MOST IMPORTANT SINGLE THING, BEYOND DISCIPLINE AND CREATIVITY IS DARING TO DARE."

— MAYA ANGELOU

"IT TAKES STRENGTH
AND COURAGE TO
ADMIT THE TRUTH."

— RICK RIORDAN

"WHATEVER YOU DO, YOU NEED COURAGE. WHATEVER COURSE YOU DECIDE UPON, THERE IS ALWAYS SOMEONE TO TELL YOU THAT YOU ARE WRONG. THERE ARE ALWAYS DIFFICULTIES ARISING THAT TEMPT YOU TO BELIEVE YOUR CRITICS ARE RIGHT. TO MAP OUT A COURSE OF ACTION AND FOLLOW IT TO AN END REQUIRES SOME OF THE SAME COURAGE THAT A SOLDIER NEEDS. PEACE HAS ITS VICTORIES, BUT IT TAKES BRAVE MEN AND WOMEN TO WIN THEM."

— RALPH WALDO EMERSON

"THE TWO HARDEST TESTS ON THE SPIRITUAL ROAD ARE THE PATIENCE TO WAIT FOR THE RIGHT MOMENT AND THE COURAGE NOT TO BE DISAPPOINTED WITH WHAT WE ENCOUNTER."

— PAULO COELHO

"IT'S NEVER THE WRONG TIME TO TELL YOU KIDS THAT YOU LOVE THEM. THEY ARE YOUR SEEDS. THEY NEED TO HEAR IT MORE THAN WE KNOW!"

—CURT THOMAS

"DON'T BE SATISFIED
WITH STORIES, HOW
THINGS HAVE GONE
WITH OTHERS. UNFOLD
YOUR OWN MYTH."

— RUMI

"COURAGE IS RESISTANCE TO FEAR, MASTERY OF FEAR - NOT ABSENCE OF FEAR."

— MARK TWAIN

"A SYMPATHETIC FRIEND CAN BE QUITE AS DEAR AS A BROTHER."

—HOMER

"COURAGE IS WHAT IT TAKES TO STAND UP AND SPEAK; COURAGE IS ALSO WHAT IT TAKES TO SIT DOWN AND LISTEN."

— WINSTON S. CHURCHILL

"I'M A FLAWED MAN WHO HAS FLAWLESS TALENT. EACH DAY IS A STRUGGLE TO GIVE THE WORLD MY BEST WHILE DEALING WITH MY OWN FLAWS!"

—CURT THOMAS

"AFTER A CERTAIN AGE EVERY MAN IS RESPONSIBLE FOR HIS FACE"

—ALBERT CAMUS

"Big jobs usually go to the men who prove their ability to outgrow small ones."

—Theodore Roosevelt

"IT IS NOT TITLES THAT MAKE MEN ILLUSTRIOUS, BUT MEN WHO MAKE TITLES ILLUSTRIOUS."

— MACHIAVELLI

"THE MEN WHO LEARN
ENDURANCE, ARE THEY
WHO CALL THE WHOLE
WORLD, BROTHER."

—CHARLES DICKENS

"AT THE END OF THE DAY, A LOVING FAMILY SHOULD FIND EVERYTHING FORGIVABLE."

—MARK V. OLSEN

"WHEN MEN SPEAK ILL OF THEE, LIVE SO AS NOBODY MAY BELIEVE THEM."

—PLATO

"THERE IS ONE KIND OF ROBBER WHOM THE LAW DOES NOT STRIKE AT, AND WHO STEALS WHAT IS MOST PRECIOUS TO MEN: TIME."

—NAPOLEON

"DOING NOTHING IS HAPPINESS FOR CHILDREN AND MISERY FOR OLD MEN."

—VICTOR HUGO

"THE MOST IMPORTANT THING A FATHER CAN DO FOR HIS CHILDREN IS TO LOVE THEIR MOTHER."

—HENRY WARD BEECHER

"UNTIL BLACKS AND WHITES SEE EACH OTHER AS BROTHER AND SISTER, WE WILL NOT HAVE PARITY. IT'S VERY CLEAR."

—MAYA ANGELOU

"WHEN A NATION'S YOUNG MEN ARE CONSERVATIVE, ITS FUNERAL BELL IS ALREADY RUNG."

—HENRY WARD BEECHER

"IF YOU EVER WANT TO KNOW HOW MAD A MAN CAN REALLY GET, MESS WITH HIS MONEY OR HIS KIDS!"

—CURT THOMAS

"KNOWLEDGE WILL GIVE YOU POWER, BUT CHARACTER RESPECT."

—BRUCE LEE

"IF THY BROTHER WRONGS THEE, REMEMBER NOT SO MUCH HIS WRONG-DOING, BUT MORE THAN EVER THAT HE IS THY BROTHER."

—EPICTETUS

"NOTHING
STRENGTHENS
AUTHORITY SO MUCH
AS SILENCE."

—LEONARDO DA VINCI

CHARACTER IS POWER.

—BOOKER T. WASHINGTON

"SOME DAYS I FEEL LIKE I'M SUPERMAN...AND THEN THERE ARE THOSE DAYS WHEN I FEEL LIKE MY BACK IS UP AGAINST THE WALL WITH THE PRESSURE OF BEING A HUSBAND, FATHER, SON, LEADER, BUSINESS-OWNER, OR JUST TRYING TO MAINTAIN BEING A 'GOOD MAN'. BEING ABLE TO HAVE AT LEAST ONE OR TWO 'REAL' BROTHERS WHO ARE REAL ENOUGH TO ADMIT THE SAME, GIVES ME A PEACE OF MIND THAT I'M NOT THE ONLY ONE IN THE STRUGGLE. IT'S SOMETHING WOMEN DON'T QUITE UNDERSTAND. BUT I LOVE MY TITLES, THERE ARE JUST 'THOSE DAYS'."

—CURT THOMAS

"YOU MUST RECOGNIZE THAT THE WAY TO GET THE GOOD OUT OF YOUR BROTHER AND YOUR SISTER IS NOT TO RETURN EVIL FOR EVIL."

—LOUIS FARRAKHAN

"THE GREATER THE POWER, THE MORE DANGEROUS THE ABUSE."

—EDMUND BURKE

"FATHERS WILL DO ANYTHING TO PUT FOOD ON THE TABLE FOR HIS FAMILY...TO INCLUDE KILLING ANOTHER MAN."

—CURT THOMAS

"ALL THE FORCES IN
THE WORLD ARE NOT
SO POWERFUL AS AN
IDEA WHOSE TIME HAS
COME."

—VICTOR HUGO

"An insecure man's mind can't rest. It's like a time bomb ticking and ready to explode at the slightest clue of dislike, hate, or jealously from someone. Sometime it's a past hurt or pain. Prayer and confronting the 'issue' helps to overcome it."

— Curt Thomas

"LIFE IS NOT ACCUMULATION, IT IS ABOUT CONTRIBUTION."

—STEPHEN COVEY

"IF YOU DON'T SEE
YOURSELF AS A
WINNER, THEN YOU
CANNOT PERFORM AS
A WINNER."

—ZIG ZIGLAR

"A MAN IS A SUCCESS IF HE GETS UP IN THE MORNING AND GOES TO BED AT NIGHT AND IN BETWEEN DOES WHAT HE WANTS TO DO."

—BOB DYLAN

"NO FAMILY IS PERFECT... WE ARGUE, WE FIGHT. WE EVEN STOP TALKING TO EACH OTHER AT TIMES. BUT IN THE END, FAMILY IS FAMILY... THE LOVE WILL ALWAYS BE THERE."

—UNKNOWN

"STRENGTH AND
GROWTH COME ONLY
THROUGH CONTINUOUS
EFFORT AND
STRUGGLE."

—NAPOLEON HILL

"MASTERING OTHERS
IS STRENGTH.
MASTERING YOURSELF
IS TRUE POWER."

—LAO TZU

"BE NOT HASTY IN THY
SPIRIT TO BE ANGRY:
FOR ANGER RESTETH
IN THE BOSOM OF
FOOLS."

— ECCLESIASTES 7:9

"KITES RISE HIGHEST AGAINST THE WIND - NOT WITH IT."

—WINSTON CHURCHILL

"DON'T BE AFRAID TO GIVE YOUR BEST TO WHAT SEEMINGLY ARE SMALL JOBS. EVERY TIME YOU CONQUER ONE IT MAKES YOU THAT MUCH STRONGER. IF YOU DO THE LITTLE JOBS WELL, THE BIG ONES WILL TEND TO TAKE CARE OF THEMSELVES."

—DALE CARNEGIE

"I WANT TO LIVE MY
LIFE SO WELL WITH MY
HEALTH, WEALTH,
SPIRITUAL, SOCIAL,
AND IDEAS UNTIL MY
3RD GENERATION
TELLS THE 4TH, 5TH,
AND SO ON ABOUT HOW
I LIVED!"

—CURT THOMAS

"I AM MY BROTHER'S KEEPER"

— UNKNOWN

"CIRCUMSTANCE DOES NOT MAKE THE MAN; IT REVEALS HIM TO HIMSELF."

— JAMES ALLEN

"One of the HARDEST things for me to do was to go to someone I HATED for years and ask them for forgiveness! I knew it wasn't right for me to hold it in but I couldn't get over the hurt. Once I told them how I felt and asked for their forgiveness, it felt like a huge weight was lifted off of my shoulders. Even though they didn't ask for me to forgive them, I did my part."

— Curt Thomas

www.CurtThomasSpeaks.com

THE MAN IN THE MIRROR

KEEP YOUR HEAD UP BROTHERS! I KNOW IT'S NOT EASY EVERYDAY BUT KEEP PUSHING!

I HOPE YOU FIND INSPIRATION FOR GOOD DAYS AND THOSE NOT SO GOOD DAYS!

LOVE YOU MY BROTHER,

—CURT THOMAS

The MAN in the MIRROR

THE MAN IN THE MIRROR

LIKE US ON FACEBOOK:

KEYWORD: CURT THOMAS MOTIVATIONAL SPEAKER

INSTAGRAM:

KEYWORD: @CURTTHOMASSPEAKS

FOLLOW ON TWITTER:

KEYWORD: @CURTSPEAKS

The MAN in the MIRROR